Among all the methods of forgiveness that I have taught or practiced over the past decades, Hoʻoponopono is surely one of the simplest and yet most powerful. In this book, Ulrich Emil Duprée manages to condense the essence of this Hawaiian forgiveness ritual in a way that makes it easily accessible to a large audience. If you're looking for a lovely introduction to Hoʻoponopono, written with the heart, this is the book for you!

Olivier Clerc, author of *The Gift of Forgiveness* and *Healing the Wounds of the Heart*

Ho'oponopono

The Hawaiian Ritual of Forgiveness

Ulrich E. Duprée

AN INNER TRADITIONS IMPRINT

Third revised edition 2023
Second edition 2014
First edition published in 2012 by Earthdancer GmbH

Ho'oponopono
The Hawaiian Ritual of Forgiveness
Ulrich Emil Duprée

This English edition © 2012, 2014, 2023 Earthdancer GmbH
English translation © 2023 JMS books LLP
Editing by JMS books LLP (www.jmseditorial.com)

Originally published in German as *Ho'oponopono, Das hawaiianische Vergebungsritual*
World © 2011, 2018 Schirner Verlag, Darmstadt, Germany

All rights reserved. No part of this book may be reprinted or reproduced or utilized in any form or by any electronic, mechanical, or other means, now known or hereafter invented, including photocopying and recording, or in any information storage or retrieval system, without permission in writing from the publisher.

Cover design: Silja Bernspitz, Schirner
Cover illustration: Marina Krasnovid (water), www.fotolia.com, Telnov Oleksii (flower illustration), Nipaporn Panyacharoen (frangipani), both shutterstock.com

Typesetting: DesignIsIdentity.com
Typeset in Minion
Printed and bound in China by Reliance Printing Co., Ltd.

Cataloging-in-Publication Data for this title is available from the Library of Congress.

ISBN 978-1-64411-880-1 (print)
ISBN 978-1-64411-881-8 (ebook)

Published by Earthdancer, an imprint of Inner Traditions
www.earthdancerbooks.com, www.innertraditions.com

Pardoning, forgiving,
and reconciling can be
learned and practiced.
A great reward awaits everyone.
I call it "healing the heart,"
and I would like to invite
you all to share in it.

Contents

The Adventure Begins — 8

What Is Hoʻoponopono? — 14
Healing with Love — 15
Solving Problems and Resolving Conflict — 21
The Power of Forgiveness — 30
A Brief Historical Overview — 42
   The Four Basic Phases of a Traditional Hoʻoponopono — 48
The Story of Ihaleakala Hew Len, PhD — 53
The Core of the Simplified Hoʻoponopono — 58
How to Find Your Part in a Hoʻoponopono — 63

The Spiritual Laws — 68
Everything Is Connected to Everything Else — 68
Everything Has a Cause and Effect — 73
Everything Is Vibration — 77
All Spirit Is God's Spirit — 81

Ho'oponopono in Practice	**88**
Relationships and Partnerships	88
Profession, Vocation, and Remuneration	92
Health	97
The Global Political Challenge	100
The Desire for Peace	**105**
For Healing	110
About the Author	*111*
Picture Credits	*112*

The Adventure Begins

This book is about forgiveness—so what better way to begin than with a dramatic story of sacrifice? It was just before Christmas 1970, when I was eight years old, that my father bled to death on the carpet in front of me. Why? How was this fair? What did it mean?

Whenever we are about to embark upon a journey, such as the journey of life itself, we have no way of knowing what will happen, and so it is only in retrospect that we can really grasp the significance of the events in our life. No doubt you have also experienced how a significant event such as a divorce or an illness can later turn out to have been beneficial or indeed even a blessing after bringing about an important turning point in your life. The low points we encounter often prove to be among the most fruitful. During my search for answers to the meaning of life I have met people who, each in their own way, have opened a new door and afforded insight into different spiritual paths: Christian teaching, gnosis (esoteric knowledge), anthroposophy, Taoism, yoga sciences, and finally *huna*. While all of these paths might appear very different at first sight, I have come to the conclusion that they are merely different productions of the same play, to use the theater as a metaphor—the one universal truth that is revealed in every age and in every culture.

I was conducting a family constellation in 2008 when one of the participants came up to me and handed me an audiobook about Ho'oponopono (and Cosmic Ordering) by Bärbel and Manfred Mohr (*Ho'oponopono, eine Methode zur Realitätsgestaltung*). He told me that I would get something out of it. I had seen the word "Ho'oponopono" before but had not given it much thought because of its odd spelling and pronunciation. After the constellation, I listened to the audiobook's introduction and then had what people call a mystical experience—one that was to be repeated. In a kind of vision, I saw four white fields melt into one. My skin seemed to be glowing, and I felt as though something was breathing right through me. I was rather taken aback, but the principles of Ho'oponopono and Huna lay spread out before me. As a Hawaiian shaman later explained, something had been reactivated within me,

and just as the right side of our brain often grasps things as a whole in a fraction of a second, the left side takes a little longer to piece things together, so I began to research, learn, and practice Hoʻoponopono.

In 2009 I wrote a book about healing oneself and the world (*Heile dich selbst, und heile die Welt*), probably the first book in German to describe in detail how to conduct the original Hoʻoponopono, the Hawaiian family ritual, using case studies and a Hawaiian glossary. I would like to use this book to introduce you, the reader, to the spirit and the concept of Hoʻoponopono and Huna in an accessible manner rather than as a dry textbook. I am deeply grateful that you have taken an interest in this book and I have no doubt that you will find a number of pearls of wisdom hidden within.

In the Hawaiian forgiveness ritual of Hoʻoponopono we are in possession of a key that can open doors in what were previously simple blank walls. That is why at this point I would like to express my thanks and deepest respect for all those throughout the world who have left behind the keys to such doors for us, and for all those who will do so in the future.

In the protected seclusion of a small archipelago in the middle of that most peaceful of oceans, the Pacific, a method of healing has survived through the ages. I would like to introduce you to this precious flower from Hawaii, a tender and delicate—indeed, holy—bloom that is also considered the most effective way of resolving conflicts and problems. Welcome to the world of Ho'oponopono.

What Is Ho'oponopono?

Ho'oponopono is a way of solving and resolving internal and external problems and conflicts while at the same time healing relationships: your relationship with yourself, with other people, and with your environment. It is one of the traditional cleansing techniques in Huna, a practical system for shaping your life in a purely positive way. *Hu* means "knowledge" and *na* is "wisdom." The keepers of these old and in some cases secret teachings are known as *kahunas* (experts in Huna).

In a Ho'oponopono we cleanse ourselves not externally but rather internally—mentally and spiritually—of destructive patterns of behavior, negative beliefs, misunderstandings, and wrongdoing. In other words, we cleanse ourselves of whatever causes problems for us and for others. At the very heart of the process is a simple and effective forgiveness ritual. This dignified and elegant method of forgiveness and reconciliation makes it possible to resolve challenges that are very personal to us, as well as conflicts within a community or group. Hoʻoponopono's very special effects are manifested in the three great spheres of our lives: our partnership and family, our professional life, and in health matters.

Healing with Love

The Hawaiian shamans (*kahunas*) believed that there is no problem that cannot be resolved with Hoʻoponopono, however apparently hopeless it may be. The reason for this is love (*aloha*), the greatest power in the universe. Just as there is no darkness in the sun, there is no negativity in love, and this is the reason why love can heal all. It steadfastly rejects all sorrow, guilt, inferiority, and destructivity. The three syllables *a-lo-ha* mean "sharing the same spiritual essence with one another." *Aloha* sees what we have in common and cleanses what divides us. We have to understand that we—you and I, and all of us—are on a common journey, and that there is a great power that unites us all, the energy of pure love, *mana aloha*. The only command in Huna is, "Never harm, always help." Following this rule begins with ourselves, of course, which is why it is very important that we forgive ourselves and let go of all the negativity that harms both us and others. Even if some don't care to admit it, perhaps because they (still) find it embarrassing to talk about their feelings, love is what everyone yearns for. It is the essence of the Source (*ke akua*), the loving divinity that permeates everything and is inherent within everything, within you and every atom. Wise Hindu monks among whom I once had the privilege of living called this love *bhakti,* "devotion," while the Tibetan monks I met knew it as "compassion." These terms may possibly result in misunderstandings, as when we talk about *aloha,* it is not simply about, for example, evoking a nice feeling but a directly perceptible energy that can influence the real world and create a new reality in our lives. Just as invisible light manifests itself in the form of many colors in a rainbow, so too does love have many facets: acceptance, listening, compassion, forgiveness, freedom from judgment and prejudice, benevolence, attention, togetherness, closeness, romance, security, common goals, gifts, and much more. All these qualities of love, of *aloha,* will help to heal a crisis in a marriage, for example, or a conflict within a group of people, a firm or company, because they lead us away from division and back toward unity. This is what we all want for ourselves. I would like to invite you to enter a protected space in which you can reconnect with yourself and experience inner peace and abundant richness.

Huna, which can also be translated as "the secret," is based on the fundamental understanding that we live in a universe of abundance (*piha pono wai wai*). You, the reader, are a perfect expression of this abundance. What stands in the way of experiencing good relationships, inner wealth, spiritual growth, material prosperity, and perfect health, however, is ourselves. Ultimately, we always know what we could improve, but something within us holds us back. This something is our unconscious, destructive thinking, and our mental programming, such as holding on to fears and worries, prejudices, feelings of inferiority, bad habits, and doubts that prevent us from experiencing our own perfection and bringing us into harmony with life and abundance. With our negative beliefs about ourselves and the world, we humans are often our own worst enemies.

Imagine you are holding a large stone in each hand. If I wanted to hand you a precious jewel, you would need to drop the stones. It is just the same with the gifts of the universe. The secret to being able to receive things is to let go of our own inner stones, of habitual judgments and patterns of behavior, and to trust that we may do so without being hurt.

Hoo (ho'o) means "to do, arrange, construct," demonstrating that it is an active principle; to have a good relationship, you have to actually *do* something. *Pono* means "correct, flexible, compassionate" and is one of the seven great principles and wisdoms of Huna, as we need flexibility and adaptability for everything in life. The generally accepted translation of Hoʻoponopono is "putting things right again." After carrying one out, everything should be back in its rightful place. The underlying principle is that everything, in both our personal lives and in the ecosystem, has a significance and therefore a place. We want to allow all things, whatever or whoever they might be, to take up their rightful position and therefore heal the relationship. When we are in the right place (for example, on our life path), life flows through us without hindrance; we then feel fulfilled and able to follow our true calling, the reason we are here.

Have you noticed that *pono* appears twice in the word Ho'oponopono? Expressed in modern terms, *pono pono* might mean something like "win-win relationships for all concerned." The aim is not to achieve a compromise but to put relationships right on every level: with ourselves, with other people, with our environment, and the natural world, and, ultimately, to heal our relationship with our spiritual Source. Huna understands that in this world everything is interconnected and therefore every problem in this world is a relationship issue that affects us as well. We have relationships with our bodies, our families, our environment, and on a global level with plant species, animals, and people about which and whom we know nothing at all but whose lives we affect and/or threaten through our consumerist behavior, among other things. As you can imagine, the possibilities for using Ho'oponopono for self-help, as a family conference, for mediation in a professional context within a company, in psychotherapy, for environmental protection, even in peace work at a diplomatic level, are potentially endless; the only boundaries are those we impose upon ourselves, as ever in our lives.

Solving Problems and Resolving Conflict

The word "problem" originally comes from the Greek *problēma*, which in the ancient world meant the gods were placing an obstruction in a person's path. The rulers of Olympus did not do this to annoy us but to challenge us to grow. Every problem, whether it is an issue with a new colleague at work, difficulty with a neighbor, a traffic jam, an illness, a relationship crisis, or a slightly malnourished bank account, is a challenge that we can accept as a lesson to be learned and an indication of what may be on the wrong track in our own lives. The people we regard as enemies because of a problem or issue we may have with them are actually helpful friends. In a Hoʻoponopono we say that each conflict is simply a reflection of a dark part of ourselves that we can still cleanse. The more you eliminate past hurt and disappointments, for example, the better you feel. When you grow personally, your situation in life, your circumstances, improve as well. As soon as you comb your hair or put on your favorite outfit, the person in the mirror instantly looks better too!

Exercise: Solve Problems

Sit back, relax, and think of a problem that has been bothering you for some time. Visualize this issue sitting on a chair opposite you. Explore your feelings. What emotions come to the fore? Breathe easily and calmly. The problem cannot harm you from the chair opposite. You and the problem are separate from one another. Think about how you are feeling and make a note of your emotions. Now say the following four sentences aloud: "I'm sorry. Please forgive me. I love you. Thank you." Remain in this position as an observer and repeat the four sentences until a sense of understanding comes to you. Thank you.

For example, when you encounter someone whose frame of mind is "pushing your buttons," perhaps a cranky colleague in a bad mood, this person is in fact revealing your own moodiness. If someone lies to you, you might ask yourself in what aspects of your life you are not being honest with or true to yourself, or when you are being insincere. If someone fails to arrive for a meeting and you have been "stood up," think about all the people you have left waiting in the past and what promises you have made to yourself and then broken. Feel regret for all these shortcomings and then forgive and make peace with yourself, in order to reach a new decision. As you move toward inner harmony, the external mirror follows your movements.

As a story from the very beginning of mankind tells us, the problems of the world arose when we strayed from the path and erred, and in place of the single force of love there were now two forces, Good and Evil. In the place of compassion and goodwill stood judgment and discrimination, and humanity took a step away from unity toward division. This was, so to speak, the first time in history that we distanced ourselves from what we are, which is perfect—perfect in spirit (in Latin, *spiritus* is "breath," "wind"). We separated ourselves from love and mercy, and have lived in rivalry with other people ever since. This concept of competition, of disunity, is the root of all envy, greed, ill will, poverty, hunger, and war.

Deep in their hearts, people mistakenly consider themselves inferior, torn this way and that, and disparage or devalue others just to make themselves look better. Use Hoʻoponopono to escape this disharmony, to return to unity from division, and to regain healthy self-regard and inner peace. The healing force in this respect is always the divine principle in your heart—the loving Source (*ke akua*) that is within you and everywhere.

The outward expression of conflict is known as *pilikia* (meaning a momentary drama or trouble) in the Hawaiian forgiveness ritual, although this is just the tip of the iceberg; the wounds (*hala*) that cause the hurt and are the actual problem lie hidden. You and I both know that our problems lie not outside us but within—in our thoughts, mistaken beliefs, and mental programming. It is not the adult in us, the rational waking consciousness (*uhane*) that suffers, but the so-called inner child, the feeling self (*unihipili*). Our inner child feels unsure and unloved. Whenever someone "presses our buttons," it is a clear indication of an old hurt that is yet to heal. Someone has reopened an old wound and it is painful. If there were no old wound hidden away inside, we would respond with calm and compassion rather than with negativity. Without feelings of hurt inside, we would help others, just as we would not chastize someone lost in the woods for their inability to find their way but instead would immediately indicate the right path.

We are used to viewing our world as a duality: rich or poor, hot or cold, up or down, like the two sides of a single coin. This is precisely how we perceive personal conflicts and international disputes in the world. We see ourselves and we see the conflict. We see the victim (that's who we think we are, either directly or indirectly) and we see the "perpetrators," and then we say, "It's their fault," by which we mean that they owe us our happiness.

It starts to get interesting when we put questions to these perpetrators, the people we hold responsible for stealing our happiness, for threatening us, and against whom we struggle or whom we avoid at work or on the street because we fear their energy. When we ask them why they act as they do, we are sure to hear that they are doing their best and had no other option. In other words, perpetrators, when criticized, similarly like to think of themselves as victims. It is our subjective view of the world and the way we think of ourselves that is revealed. In Huna this principle is known as *huna ike* ("I am what I think I am"). People justify themselves, which is where Ho'oponopono comes into play in couples' therapy, social work, and in mediation. In a Ho'oponopono all those involved in a particular issue ask themselves how they have contributed to the problem, bringing to an end the trading of blame and accusation. No one seeks to place blame on others but instead each person works on self-cleansing. Everyone follows this system in a Ho'oponopono and works toward a common goal—such as saving a partnership or marriage, a contract, a business, or the rainforest—and powerful synergies are created. No one is rejected, but instead all pull together (*ponopono*).

Essentially, a Ho'oponopono challenges us to step out of our role as victim and to take responsibility for our own emotions and our own lives, instead of leaving everything to people we may not greatly respect. Thanks to this change of perspective, we instantly regain the power to actively shape our own lives. All our moaning, complaining, and attempts at self-justification cease and we remove the breeding ground for other destructive emotions with the power to destroy us and others.

In Huna and Ho'oponopono this is known as *ike pono mea,* meaning "everything is essentially always fine," as we ourselves decide if we want to be surrounded by love or by drama in life.

Exercise: Resolve Conflict

Sit back in your chair, relax, and think of a person about whom you may have reservations, someone you avoid, fail to get on with or have some dispute with. Explore your emotions and consider how you are feeling. Put yourself in the position of an observer. Observe yourself, and describe your feelings as precisely as possible. What are the three primary emotions you are experiencing? Now sum up your feelings in just a few words ("I feel fear, sorrow, anger, helplessness . . .").

Say aloud: "I feel/have a sense of . . . [name your feeling]."

Breathe in a calm, even rhythm and say aloud: "Just as I have these feelings, this person has no doubt also experienced . . . [name your feeling]. Just like me, this person experiences . . . [name the three negative emotions you feel]. I feel with them. I'm sorry. They are suffering, and I am suffering. I now forgive myself for any negativity that I may have toward . . . [say the first name of the person with whom you have an issue]. I forgive them too. We seem to have something in common. I love myself, and I love (respect, esteem) you. I give thanks for everyone's healing in this moment." Repeat this exercise and remain in your position as an observer. Thank you.

We must develop compassion on the path to forgiveness. This may not be easy, but the exercise above may help you to recognize that even those who deliberately hurt others are suffering, deep in their hearts. People who steal from others, abuse or humiliate them, or destroy their environment, driven by greed, are ignorant of the consequences of their actions and are at an immature stage in their personal growth and awareness. While a mature person looks out for the well-being of others, immature people, driven by ego, are concerned only with what is good for them, but why waste energy on feeling anger or rage at them? Instead, we should feel sorry for them, just as we feel compassion for a crying child.

Peace begins within me.

The Power of Forgiveness

Having troubling thoughts about past events does not make this world and our lives any better. The opposite proves to be true when old wounds continue to fester inside like a smoldering fire. A toxic mental cocktail of negative emotions, such as anger, helplessness, and feeling overburdened or a victim, will make us gloomy and sad. Admittedly, we have known for centuries of the destructive effects of negative emotions on the body (known as psychosomatics), but people still fall into the trap of thinking that they will feel better at some point if they hang on to the feelings of anger, sorrow, or sense of self-sacrifice long enough.

Two itinerant monks arrived at a river beside which a young woman was seated. The woman said to them: "I can't swim; if you wish to cross this river, oh Wise Ones, I would be grateful if one of you could carry me across." One of the monks immediately said, "Come and climb upon my shoulders," and together, all three of them crossed safely at a ford in the river. Once on the other side, the young woman bade them farewell and the two monks continued their journey. They walked in silence, but something seemed to be bothering one of them. "What is it, my friend? You seem upset," said the one who had carried the girl. The other monk then chided him, saying: "You are stupid, how could you touch a woman? We are monks and we live in seclusion." The other responded: "It's true, I carried the woman. But I put her down on the other side; as far as I can tell, you seem to be carrying her still."

Without being aware of it, some of us carry our disappointments from the past into the present. By replaying a troubling event in our thoughts, we suffer twice: when the hurtful event initially occurs and then again when it is relived in our memory. In this way, imperceptibly but ultimately, we become the perpetrator by burdening both ourselves and others, shifting responsibility for such sorrow onto the circumstances at the time of the event or onto other people. And yet who is returning to the past, who is doing the thinking and feeling? The perpetrators rarely care about our feelings because they are generally only interested in their own. It is up to us to pay attention to our own emotions.

Exercise: Forgive Your Past Mistakes

Option A

1. Think of a mistake or blunder for which to this day you have been unable to forgive yourself. Imagine this mistake placed on a chair opposite you. Look at it. If it were an object, what color would it be? What shape and size might it have? Honor your mistake as a contributor to your learning journey. (Don't think you could have avoided it—if you hadn't already made this mistake, it would still be waiting for you.) Now be sure to forgive yourself for having been annoyed about it for so long.

2. What did you learn from this? Make a note of three things that show you have become wiser because of your mistake and be thankful. The ability to find something positive in every problem is an indication of an emotionally mature personality.

3. This troubling and stressful incident belongs to the past, so let it drift away on its chair and recede into the background down an imaginary

road until it has reached what seems to be an appropriate distance. Now observe it from afar. What does that do to you? Send it even farther away until it is a mere dot on the horizon and dismiss it.

Option B
1. Think of a mistake or blunder in your past for which you have still been unable to forgive yourself. Imagine yourself sitting on a chair opposite you. The person (this second, other you) sitting opposite is yourself at the age you were when you made the mistake. Go backward and forward in time, observing yourself at different ages, as if you were focusing the lens or adjusting the zoom on a camera.

2. Now look at yourself without judgment; you were younger and less experienced back then. Be aware that you must be compassionate and that only you can give yourself this absolution. Accept yourself completely and be whole again. Say aloud: "I'm sorry for judging and condemning you. You were only doing your best and I accept you. Please forgive me. I love you. I love

you with all my heart. Thank you for our healing on every level."

3. Mentally merge with and embrace your imagined self. Focus on this self-embrace for at least seven minutes. This exercise, one of the simplest methods of self-healing in the Huna tradition, is known in Hawaiian as *oulu oulu*. Several of the so-called "happiness" hormones, including serotonin and oxytocin, are released during this self-embrace, both reducing levels of the stress hormone cortisol and boosting your immune system.

Forgiveness is a therapeutic key that enables us to close the door on, and come to terms with, the past. It allows us to open up to a happy future. Forgiveness is, of course, not intended to right wrongs but to be a gift that you give yourself. Forgiveness frees us from an emotional burden that we have no desire to bear. Who wants to drag around old conflicts, like a sack of stones, for the rest of their life? In the same way, forgiveness is not about encouraging us to, for example, get involved with any unpleasant people in our circle. Quite the opposite: when we cleanse ourselves of our feelings of guilt, we are no longer in danger of sacrificing ourselves or acting against our own values.

A camel was drinking water at a river when it heard a scorpion say: "Oh, my dear camel, I have to cross to the other side of the river. My aunt is sick and she is expecting me. Only I can help her in her hour of need, as I know how to make soup properly. Camels are the best swimmers for miles around. Please have mercy and take me across." "Hmm. You're a scorpion. I'm worried that if I let you onto my back to bring you across, you will sting me and I will die," answered the camel. The scorpion replied: "How could you think that of me? If we are in the middle of the river and I sting you, I'll drown too. Trust me, I need you." Upon these emollient words, the camel knelt down and the scorpion scrambled up onto one of its humps. The camel waded into the river. They got talking, and the scorpion told lots of stories about its family. When the camel and the scorpion were in the middle of the river, the scorpion flashed its sting in the sun and stung with all its might. Grimacing with pain, the camel asked, "Why did you do that? Now we are both going to die!" The scorpion replied, "I'm a scorpion—it's in my nature."

As this fable illustrates, we are able to forgive a person their nature and actions while still firmly refusing to have anything to do with them. In such instances, it is important to eliminate any feelings of guilt or self-reproach that might lead you to offer yourself as a victim.

Those who have learned to forgive themselves and others describe how they feel they have taken a great step forward in their personal growth, and in every aspect of their professional lives and even in their health. This great act of letting go reduces stress, one of the principal causes of illness. Many therapists already equate forgiveness with healing. Indeed, life itself heals and forgives: when you cut your finger, for example, the body's innate powers of self-healing immediately kick into action and a scab begins to form over the wound. Forgiveness does not demand any form of retribution or revenge, but it forgives our inattention and grants us the freedom to learn from this unfortunate experience. Both physical and mental wounds will heal if we do not deliberately keep them open. This is why, at the end of the forgiveness ritual, we say that the matter is *oki* and *pani*, "dealt with and off the table." There is no reason to pick over what has happened, but instead we should turn our attention to our goals and find the common ground. We have let go of the past with love, and together with the present and the future, it has been returned to its proper place.

In the same way that we learn how to do fundamental things like walking and talking as a young child, the act of pardoning, forgiving, and reconciling with something can also be learned and practiced. Some people are quick to take this on board and master it, while others require a little more time, but a great reward awaits everyone. For me it is "healing the heart," and I would like to invite you to do this, to send a new and powerful impulse and introduce a new vibration into your life. First and foremost, decide to forgive and love yourself unconditionally. If you cannot do this straight away, start by simply pretending that you have done so and make it into an affirmation. At first, repeating a sentence such as "I am beautiful and my body shape is good" might sound completely absurd, but eventually you will be able to feel and see it too, and, interestingly, other people will also see this echo of our inner image, our vision of ourselves. And just like a mirror, other people show us what we think of and feel about ourselves deep in our hearts, in our subconscious. Therefore, if you feel that people are avoiding you, for example, ask yourself which aspects of yourself you are still rejecting. Is it your body, a particular habit, or your past? We can't expect others to love us if we have still not forgiven ourselves for something.

The act of bullying, in particular, is something that can be solved with Ho'oponopono. Since the world is a mirror of our inner processes, pollution of the environment is a reflection of the pollution of our hearts, and all war is an echo of the violence that lies within us. For this reason, one of the fundamental practices in Huna and Ho'oponopono is to connect with and accept yourself unconditionally, and once you are sustained in this way, to grow and develop on a personal level. Love for others can only flow from this love of ourselves. The more we heal ourselves as individuals—you, me, us—the more this world will heal from the wounds it has suffered at the hands of humanity.

Exercise: Self-Love

In future, when you go to the bathroom, make a point of regularly greeting your reflection with a cheery "Aloha," "Hello," or "Namaste." Stand in front of the mirror every morning and say with conviction, repeating it ten times in total:

"I love you, [your first name]. I'm sorry that I paid you so little attention in the past. Please forgive me, dear [your first name]. I love you with all my heart, [your first name]. Thank you. Thank you. Thank you."

You might not see results straight away and could even feel rather angry or sad—after all, remember that you are also addressing your "inner child" (*unihipili*), your wounded, emotional (and possibly also rejected) self, and the child will react. If you have neglected yourself, perhaps for years on end, it is difficult to suddenly do an about-turn and instantly love yourself from that moment on. We become used to our habits and need to adjust to seeing ourselves in love. Make loving yourself a habit. This is not egotistical but merely sensible. Do you want to live or work with people who do not love themselves? Forget these outdated attitudes and misunderstandings! Thinking negatively about ourselves and other people is just a habit, while abandoning this way of thinking is part and parcel of developing a higher consciousness.

> Please remember that you are the person with whom you have been allowed to be until the end of your life, so begin, right now (*manawa*), to forgive yourself, to like and love yourself. Just like driving a car, it all depends on which way you are steering. Like your car, you will travel in the direction in which your wheels are pointing and, in the same way, everything in your life will turn out for the good if you can be patient enough to remain on the path of love.

People generally understand forgiveness as the act of a victim forgiving the perpetrator, the person who has harmed them or caused an issue. In a Hawaiian forgiveness ritual, there is mutual pardoning, forgiveness, and absolution on four relationship levels: victim–perpetrator; perpetrator–victim; perpetrator–perpetrator; and victim–victim. The perpetrator forgives the victim and the victim also forgives the perpetrator. In conflicts and disputes in particular, these roles are purely subjective, and people who are perpetrators often feel they have been provoked to act. In a Hoʻoponopono, the ultimate goal is to cleanse all negative emotions forever, and so forgiving others is followed by forgiving yourself. Therefore, the victim and the perpetrator now forgive themselves; this part of the ritual is so important because in it we let go of all the feelings of guilt that hold us back in life and constantly attract new perpetrators, like bait on a hook. This phase of mutually requesting forgiveness is known as *mihi*, and the granting of forgiveness is called *kalana* ("freedom" and "rekindling the light of love").

An old Hawaiian song compares the heart to a bowl in which a soft, gentle light burns: the flame of love (*aloha*). Anything is possible with and through this love—flying with birds or swimming with sharks, metaphorically speaking. However, every time someone is angry or envious, it is as if they place a stone in their bowl. This stone drives out the light, and with each additional stone of envy, greed, or anger, the heart becomes darker. When the heart is heavy and your strength is flagging, flying with birds and swimming with sharks becomes impossible. You must turn the bowl upside down and let the stones fall out, so that the light of love, the flame of *aloha,* will then burn as brightly, gently, and brilliantly as before and everything becomes possible once again.

A Brief Historical Overview

Haleaka Iolani Pule, the Hawaiian priestess and *kahuna hoʻoponopono,* told me that the origins of Hoʻoponopono lie far back in the past. Ancient songs and stories date its emergence to around 5,700 years ago, and therefore, interestingly, to a time described in ancient Sanskrit texts such as the Ayurveda as the beginning of the "era of conflict." This new and threatening zeitgeist was felt elsewhere around the world, so it is no coincidence that biblical chronology also begins here. Time had moved on, striking a new hour for humankind. We had stepped beyond the inner paradise of the unity of all being, and had begun to envy one another, with all the associated consequences: insatiable greed, ruthlessness, cruelty, theft, robbery, and even murder.

When the *ohana,* the Hawaiian family, gathered each evening, to listen to old stories, to dance, and to heal, they would tell one another about the day's events. They would speak about their encounters with Nature, the Great Mother. They respected everything that exists with humility, venerating the powerful ocean, the mighty rocks, volcanoes, and the elements. In order to maintain peace, they would always discuss any quarrels or disputes, any reservations one person may have had about something, negative feelings, misunderstandings, and any improper behavior toward people, animals, and Nature. Nothing was held back, everything would be resolved that same evening in love and forgiveness, absolution and reconciliation. This allowed their fellowship and community to blossom and, by the following day, they had no reason to reproach one another and everyone felt secure.

Over the centuries, from these gatherings at which the conflicts between clan members could be resolved and the community strengthened, a ritual developed that at some point came to be known as Hoʻoponopono, meaning "putting things right again." In the 1950s the Hawaiian elder Mary Kawena Pukui (1895–1986) described this original traditional Hoʻoponopono as a kind of family therapy, a method of correcting improper behavior among relatives. It consisted of four phases led by a mediator (*haku*) who supported both the parties in conflict and the *ohana* during the resolution process. After offering communal prayers and making a connection with the ancestors (*pule*), a discussion phase (*mahiki*) followed. In the third phase (known as *mihi*), everyone, including the perpetrator, the victim, and the audience (*hihia*), asked for absolution and forgiveness. In the final phase, known as *kalana*, meaning "freedom" and/or "rekindling the light," all anger, resentment, and discord were erased forever with the granting of unconditional forgiveness. Where resentment and bad temper had previously made the hearts of the participants cold and dark, and the light of love had almost been extinguished, the warming flame of *aloha* now burned again. Once the light had been rekindled, everyone could see clearly and say: "Aloha. I see and respect the Divine within you."

Some twenty years later, in the 1970s, the *kahuna* Morrnah Nalamaku Simeona (1913–1992) reintroduced Ho'oponopono as a ritual for resolving all kinds of conflicts and disputes. Making use of Christian and Indian influences, she adapted the traditional Ho'oponopono to the modern world. Since then individuals have been able to conduct the ritual as a kind of mental and spiritual self-help treatment. Morrnah Simeona brought into it the concept of the three selves: the higher self, middle self, and lower self (*aumakua, uhane, unihipili*). The focus was placed on carrying out twelve individual steps, complemented with prayers and dedication rituals. After her death, Ihaleakala Hew Len, PhD, her former pupil, took over the reins of her Foundation of I, refining it as Self I-Dentity through Ho'oponopono®. He taught Ho'oponopono as a method of cleansing memories (known as "data") that are obstacles to spiritual identity.

Every so often, people promote one system or another as the "true Ho'oponopono." When asked about this, the Hawaiian priestess Haleaka Iolani Pule replied: "All the variants are like leaves on a tree. With Ho'oponopono, it's not a question of who is right, it's about good relationships." I try to follow this message from a *kahuna* and teach the different variations.

It can be difficult to say "I love you" and to pray in certain environments (in a corporate setting, for example), but even there the spirit of Hoʻoponopono can still be at work, providing people agree to respect Nature and their co-workers. It follows, therefore, that a different Hoʻoponopono would be conducted in a school setting than for a marital dispute, and so on.

The Four Basic Phases of a Traditional Hoʻoponopono

Mary Kawena Pukui emphasizes that all four phases must be carried out each time, and that no single phase constitutes a Hoʻoponopono on its own.

Pule: connection with the Source *(ke akua)* and the ancestors *(aumakua).*
Mahiki: the discussion phase and finding the part everyone has played in the problem *(pilikia, hala, hihia).*
Mihi: mutual pardoning, forgiveness, and absolution.
Kala (Kalana): letting go, giving thanks, and the closing prayer.

These four phases are like the four seasons, and break down into twelve individual steps.

1. *Pule* is the introductory prayer, calling upon the ancestors and/or the Source. It lays a powerful foundation for a successful beginning of the Hoʻoponopono, asking for wisdom, support, understanding, and correct listening and speaking. Thanks are given for the opportunity to be close to one another in understanding, to give and receive love, and for the power of forgiveness.

2. *Kūkulu kumuhana* is the preparatory step and a mutual blessing. All the participants are welcomed into the group and any resistance to the process is set aside. The objective of resolving the individual or the group's problem in love is affirmed and summarized.

3. *Hala* is the specific problem, such as a breach of an agreement or of rules, a misunderstanding, a transgression or crime. *Hala* is sometimes barely expressible in words and is therefore also known as *pilikia,* "the drama."

4. *Hihia* represents the different levels of the problem, their effects, and the many ways they can be expressed. Everything that upsets, annoys, and confuses us is a sign that we are not at peace with ourselves and that something in us needs to be set right once more. This "something" is our part in the conflict, the way in which we contributed to it.

5. *Mahiki* is discussion of the problem, during which the participants speak about what they see, hear, and feel. They speak about their own needs and the needs of the group. The conversation is a process of self-discovery, with the participants looking within themselves and seeking their true motives.

6. *Manaʻo* is when each participant objectively communicates their feelings, motivations, emotions, perceptions, and needs, so that all those involved can understand how things evolved and worked out in the way that they did.

7. *Hoʻomalu* is a period of "time-out" for calm and introspection, a resting period that is especially important when the participants' frustrations and

unfulfilled expectations and wishes are too great and the proceedings get heated.

8. *Mihi* is the heartfelt confession of having done something destructive and hurt others. It is the inner effort to restore peace and clarity by asking for forgiveness.

9. *Kala* means freeing yourself from all destructive feelings and wasting no more time on judging others or on retaliation and feelings of resentment or envy, and so on. It is a transformation process through which we set ourselves free from the past. *Kala* is the granting of forgiveness.

10. *Oki* means "dealt with," hence the problem has been resolved and is now "off the table." There is no need to bring it up again, it is now with the loving Source.

11. *Pani* means "to stir." This is a closing summary and a reinforcement of the aims of the individual or group. After all, a Hoʻoponopono would be of little use if all those involved continued to behave as before.

12. *Pule hoʻopau* is the closing prayer, thanking the Source and the ancestors for having given all those involved the understanding, intelligence, and wisdom to actively contribute to the solution. Traditionally, a Hoʻoponopono is then brought to a conclusion by sharing a meal.

The Story of Ihaleakala Hew Len, PhD

As early as the 1950s, Erika Haertig, an American doctor, was already hailing Ho'oponopono as probably the most effective way of resolving problems and conflicts ever conceived by any one culture. Just how effective it is was demonstrated thirty years later by Ihaleakala Hew Len, PhD, in his healing of mentally ill prisoners in Hawaii. Since then the story has spread worldwide via the internet and has helped to herald a great rise in awareness of Ho'oponopono in both North and South America, as well as in Europe.

In 1983 Hew Len was asked by an acquaintance to work in the psychiatric ward of the state prison at Kaneohe in Hawaii, where more than thirty mentally ill prisoners were being held. There was a shortage of prison staff for good reason, as the institution and the work there were both frequently described as hellish. Hence the hiring and then retention of staff was a major problem and many would quit as soon as they realized just how challenging the place was. Hew Len proved to be the exception. He consented to join the team providing he could use a healing method that he had just discovered. Yet he would only read the prisoners' medical histories, he would not speak to the inmates themselves.

So what did Hew Len do? Over the ensuing four years, he read the prisoners' reports several times a day, asking himself: "What darkness, what negativity, what violence is within me, that something like this exists in my world? What part have I played in my brother in spirit having committed his crime?" Whenever he found some aspect of this within himself, in his heart (such as violence, aggression, hatred, revenge, envy, jealousy—in other words, the whole gamut of the depths to which human nature can sink), he conducted a Hoʻoponopono in the Hawaiian tradition and summed it up with the following:

> I'm sorry.
> Please forgive me.
> I love you.
> Thank you.

If he read in a prisoner's notes that they had robbed a store, for example, Hew Len would ask himself if he too had ever stolen or appropriated something in the broadest sense; had he taken something from himself, from other people, or from Nature? He also thought long and hard about what circumstances might cause him to raid a store or steal something, and conducted a Ho'oponopono for every instance that occurred to him.

In this way, he worked exclusively on cleansing his heart and his consciousness (*nou nou*) for months, and after he had been carrying out Ho'oponopono for a year and a half, the mood and the atmosphere in the prison hospital changed. After eighteen months no prisoner was wearing handcuffs, the sickness rate among the prison staff, warders, and therapists had reduced, and they even began to enjoy coming to work. At this point, it became possible to conduct therapeutic consultations with the prisoners and after four years, all but two of the inmates had been cured and the facility was then closed.

Did Hew Len heal anyone? Those involved would definitely say so, but he stated in an interview that he had worked only on cleansing himself and expunging "data" from his subconscious. He did not mention healing once, instead emphasizing that resolution of the particular conflict had succeeded because he had taken full responsibility for the presence of the prisoners in his life. In Ho'oponopono we step outside our habitual roles of perpetrator/victim and ask ourselves: "What is there within me that has helped to create this situation?" We take on responsibility, as it were, for a problem that crops up in our lives. I always have some share or part in a negative situation, otherwise it would not be in my life. In the West, responsibility is often and mistakenly equated with a confession of guilt, but responsibility is simply the answer to saying to oneself, in relation to one's own life: Here is an issue. What do I make of it?

Understand now that you are no longer the victim of a situation, but instead have the ability and power to solve your problems and steer your life in a new and positive direction. The cause of all our problems lies within us, as does the power to solve them. I would now like to invite you to take part in a simplified Ho'oponopono with this small book, making use of the four sentences of peace, as I call them.

The Core of the Simplified Ho'oponopono

I'm sorry. Please forgive me. I love you. Thank you.
These four short sentences seem to crystallize from thoughts and conversations after working through the four steps (*pule, mahiki, mihi,* and *kala*) of Ho'oponopono consciously and with awareness. I am including the four sentences in this book as a kind of framework, and to also give you an idea of how to use them to describe your part in proceedings, to apologize, to ask for forgiveness, and to grant forgiveness. It is sometimes even possible to achieve great success and to begin to transform destructive forces just with these four sentences alone, before conducting a full traditional Ho'oponopono.

Over the past five years, I have had the opportunity on three occasions to present lectures to, in total, around three hundred scientists, medical doctors, therapists, and practitioners in the fields of quantum physics and information medicine. This is where the phenomena attributed to Ho'oponopono find a modern explanation: the observer or their consciousness is the factor that creates reality from possibility. Everything changes in our lives when we change something within ourselves. Situations change when we look at them from another point of view (*makia*), and, in particular, when we regard them with love. This does not involve naïveté but rather the heart. Instead of seeing something as a threat, we first take a step back, connect with the source of healing (*ke akua*), and open up to new possibilities. We swap roles, see things through a perpetrator's eyes, ask ourselves how we are similar, and finally ask to wipe away the stain from our supposedly clean slate. It is just as Jesus of Nazareth taught his disciples: "And why beholdest thou the mote that is in thy brother's eye, but considerest not the beam that is in thine own eye?"

As soon as something annoys you, whenever you feel like turning around and running away from a situation, and especially whenever someone is "pushing your buttons," please join me in first saying to yourself:

> I'm sorry.
> Please forgive me.
> I love you.
> Thank you.

What do these four sentences mean?

I'm sorry.
I accept what is negative within me. I realize that we are suffering and that connects me with my feelings and with you. I or my ancestors have also caused suffering in the world, and I am sorry for that. I'm sorry if I or my ancestors have hurt you or your ancestors, either consciously or unconsciously. I regret it and I apologize.

Please forgive me.
Please forgive me for hurting you or your ancestors. I forgive myself for transgressing against the cosmic laws of harmony and love. Please forgive me for judging you (or the situation) and disrespecting our spiritual identity and our ties in the past. I ask you to forgive me for being part of the problem. I forgive myself because I feel guilty. I also forgive myself for making myself available as a victim. I also forgive myself for being a perpetrator. I forgive the perpetrator and set us free. I now forgive myself unconditionally.

I love you.
I love you, and I love myself. I recognize and respect the Divine within me and you. I love and accept the

situation just as it is. I love myself and you unconditionally, with all our weaknesses and faults. I love that which is. I trust that this situation will move me forward. I respect the situation that is showing me what needs to be done. I love the situation that has come to me in order to return me to the flow of life.

Thank you.

Thank you for divine wisdom. Thank you for divine mercy. Thank you for insight. Thank you, because I understand that the miracle of healing is already on its way to me. I thank you for the transformation of my issue or concern. I thank you, because what I have received is what I have deserved through the law of cause and effect. Thank you, because, through the power of forgiveness, I am set free from the energetic chains (*aka*) of the past. Thank you for allowing me to recognize this and that I am connected to the Source of all being. Thank you for the transformation and the insight. Thank you for the experience I have undergone. Thank you for the best solution for me and for all those involved. I allow healing to take place. I thank you for the miracle. I thank you for my life.

In saying the words thank you, we are giving permission for healing and for erasing the "data" that led to the conflict. We say thank you when we receive something. As it is impossible to fully concentrate on two things at once, our feeling of gratitude will immediately lead us from (a sense of) lack to (a sense of) abundance. Simply saying thank you means believing or being convinced that you have already received something.

How to Find Your Part in a Hoʻoponopono

It may perhaps come as a surprise to learn that on Hawaii in centuries past a Hoʻoponopono would even be held in the event of a murder. The special aspects of this method of conflict resolution are its systematic approach in four phases (*pule, mahiki, mihi, kala*) and in the way the roles of perpetrator and victim are reversed in the discussion phase. This is what makes the ritual of particular interest for mediation. In a Hoʻoponopono the victim asks: "If I had behaved like the perpetrator, why would I have done that? Why and when would I have behaved like the perpetrator?" It is important to understand that this is not an analysis of the perpetrator's motives, but rather a search for one's own potential motivations.

Similarly, the perpetrator will ask: "How would I feel as a victim? And how might I have indirectly brought this situation into my life?"

These questions lead us to the destructive aspects of our own personalities, the hurt (sometimes originating in early childhood) separating us from others that keeps us small and helpless, and so inhibits us from living out the life for which we are truly destined.

They show us, for example, when we have been envious, aggressive, or perhaps gloating, and situations in which we have refused to help others or have been unfair. They make us aware of the parts of us that we try to disguise, disown, and therefore criticize in others in order to distract from our own inability to cooperate. We recognize our incapacity for true closeness, for an equally committed partnership (bonding), or for contributing toward mutual success (win-win relationships).

Exercise: Self-Reflection

Whenever you have an issue (a problem, *pilikia*), ask yourself: "What is there about me that is the opposite of love and is causing me to have this issue? What still needs to be healed in me that is causing me to encounter this issue? What negative potential is there within me that has caused the other person to choose the path they have taken? When do I behave in a similar way? What is being mirrored to me here? What needs to be healed?" Now feel regret that you have brought negativity into the world and say with heartfelt sincerity, "I'm sorry. Please forgive me."

This repentance will bring the strength that will enable you to behave differently in future.

An example

Andy lives on the first floor of an apartment block. A couple who own several dogs live directly below. Instead of taking the dogs outside to "do their business," they only let them out onto the terrace and Andy can no longer use his balcony due to the unpleasant smell that has resulted. He has had no joy talking to his neighbors so far, and he is not happy with the situation. In fact, he thinks it stinks!

Working through the questions above we arrive at additional ones, this time aimed at ourselves, acting as a mirror image and forcing us to examine our own behavior and motivation: What do I think stinks, and what do I continually tell other people (who have to listen to things that might "get up their nose")? Where, how, and when do I poison the air? What fear, complacency, laziness or ignorance is there within me? Why and when do I overstep the boundaries of my neighbors (or those of anyone else with whom I share this planet)? Which emotions or experiences are preventing me from talking to others calmly and in a way in which they will understand my needs and take them seriously? Am I harboring old feelings of guilt that are preventing me from taking legal action? What needs of other people, the natural world, and the environment am I neglecting? In what areas of my life am I living in filth? What kind of litter am I leaving behind on the metaphorical terrace of life? Where do I pollute the air—even in a figurative sense? Where have I accepted responsibility but not followed through on the obligation?

Make a note of your answers. Think about how you feel and, after each one, say: "I am sorry for this. Please forgive me. I love you. Thank you."

The Spiritual Laws

Everything Is Connected to Everything Else

As I write this book, I am sitting beside the ocean. I can smell and taste the salt of the sea in the air and I find myself wondering where the water in my body may have come from. We ingest water simply by drinking it and through the food we eat, of course, but where might this water have originated—the Atlantic Ocean or the Pacific? And where might all the molecules that make up our bodies have once been? Perhaps your body contains some atoms that were once part of one of my ancestors, or of Julius Caesar or Nefertiti—who knows? Everything on Earth is part of the material of this planet, and just as we are connected in the physical realm, so there is a connection between our subtle bodies, our spirits. Our consciousness is a part of the omnipresent and all-pervading world spirit, and our subconscious is part of the collective subconscious. Thanks to the findings of quantum physics, we now know that everything in the cosmos is connected to everything else—right now, in this moment in which the tiniest components of reality, quantum particles, are connected by a field that is independent of time and space. The whole of Nature (humans, animals, and plants) comes from one Source and these are just different expressions of a single, all-pervading energy.

Exercise: Equal Worth

"Judge not, that ye be not judged." Matthew 7:1

Sit back, relax, and let your thoughts run free. When do you feel better, more sublime, more human, more respected than other people? When is it that you feel more attractive, smarter, and simply different, perhaps a cut above the rest because the others "simply have no idea?" Visualize the typical situations in which you elevate yourself above other people and judge them. Now carry out a Hoʻoponopono and ask forgiveness of all the people that you have laughed at and belittled over the years. As a second step, also conduct a Hoʻoponopono and ask your inner child for forgiveness for all the times you criticized and judged yourself, and especially when you felt inferior. Forgive yourself for having weakened yourself with your own condemnation, and in so doing distanced yourself from your mission in life, the reason why you are here—to heal and to bless the world through your existence. Say: "I'm sorry for judging and condemning others. I'm sorry I considered others inferior because I felt so inferior myself. I ask forgiveness for this and for weakening the overall field of consciousness. I forgive myself now. I forgive myself for all judgmental thoughts. I ask forgiveness of all those whom I have hurt with my judgment. I now unconditionally forgive all those who have hurt me because they considered themselves inferior and were therefore judgmental. I love myself. I am of great worth and I now acknowledge the great worth of every living thing. I give thanks for the healing of all those involved in the here and now. I thank you for this insight."

Thank you. You have just made a contribution to world peace.

In a Hoʻoponopono the aspect of connectedness is accounted for in the concept of *ohana,* the family. *Ohana* means "several plants with a common root." If we go back far enough, we all have common roots and, as the great family of humanity, we also have a common inheritance, namely the task of preserving this planet. All these thoughts of deep commonality are also expressed in the first phase, *pule* (connection, prayer), when the *ohana* (the family, a group, colleagues . . .) gather together, recall their common values, connect with the Source, and decide to heal an issue or conflict with empathy, emotional intelligence, and love.

Therefore, the more aware we are of this connectedness, the more successful the Hoʻoponopono will be. One of the benefits of our technological connectivity in the modern world is that seminar participants have sometimes received a friendly text, even on the same day, from the person with whom, in their thoughts, they have conducted a Hoʻoponopono.

Kahuna studies and Huna describe connections forming through *aka* threads. *Aka* is the Hawaiian term for what could be termed a sticky, ethereal substance consisting of thought that builds up between people when they think about one another. The more they think, and the more intensely, the thicker and stronger these threads become and therefore the more difficult they are to sever. When we are in love, we are constantly thinking of the wonderful person that is the object of our affections, perhaps with butterflies in our stomach, yet when someone has done us wrong, we may also be constantly thinking of that person. The perpetrator/victim relationship is like an inverted love relationship, which is why I would advise ending any such connection, as threads soon turn into strings, then cords, and eventually thick ropes. Just as it is difficult simply to forget a loving relationship, it can be tricky to forgive a perpetrator and yourself. However, you can learn to do so with the four phases of a Ho'oponopono.

Meditation

I'm sorry for paying so much attention to the person who did me wrong—devoting more attention to them than to myself or my real friends. I am changing that now. I forgive myself completely and I set the perpetrator free and in so doing I too am freed. I now forgive all those who have caused me harm, and also ask forgiveness of everyone I have hurt, knowingly or otherwise. I thank you for this insight and for the healing of all those involved.

Everything Has a Cause and Effect

We live in a universe of cause and effect, the grandfather of all laws, so to speak. This fundamental law of causality is known in Hawaiian and in Huna as *ka ua mea*. Everything is rooted in this, strung like pearls on a necklace in an eternal sequence of cause and effect.

It keeps the cosmos (from the Greek *kósmos*: harmony, order) in a state of flux and therefore also in balance. On the physical plane, it ensures the eternal transformation of substances, and on the spiritual level it ensures our learning. There is no such thing as coincidence, therefore everything, including all the problems in our lives, has a cause and consequently a meaning that can be decoded in a Hoʻoponopono. Always be proactive in asking yourself what the issues in your life are trying to tell you and what you can learn from this.

No desire, no thought, word, or deed is ever in vain. They always have some worth and possess an energetic value, a frequency and/or information that will have an effect somewhere, at some time. In the end, no energy is ever lost in the universe but merely transforms into something else. Our thoughts and deeds are like stones dropped into water, creating ripples that form the shore and the land. Everything we do and neglect to do, such as refusing someone our help, has an effect and, in turn, becomes a cause that will manifest itself in our own lives. Our inner dialogue (whether we love or criticize ourselves, or feel guilty . . .) will leave its mark on our bodies, for example, in the smile lines around our eyes or our worry lines and wrinkles, in an ache in the back or a stomach ulcer. As a first step, we must forgive ourselves for our wrongdoing and mistakes, and, as a second, correct matters. This self-forgiveness is also important for the victim. How often do we reproach ourselves for being stupid enough to let something happen? When everything is back in its rightful place, love can flow and wounds can heal.

As far as our personal life circumstances are concerned, we reap all that has been sown by ourselves or by our ancestors at one time or another. This might not be a very pleasant concept to take on board, but it reminds us to take a moment and consider our own behavior. The notion of a punishing God is alien to scientists, rational philosophers, and *kahunas* alike. For a spiritualist, the Source of all being is pure love (*mana aloha*). Crime and punishment do not exist within the Divine because it has limitless love for itself and its creation. There is no negativity of any kind within the Divine Source, but in order to correct our behavior, there is the principle of causality. So people punish themselves through their sins and by sowing negativity that they will eventually reap. When someone touches a hot oven, we can safely assume that there will be consequences. In the same way, we should draw conclusions from the problems in our lives and then cleanse the causes in a Ho'oponopono. Our problems are essentially symptoms of energetic tension arising from an injustice, and times when giving and taking were not in harmony. This wrongdoing has resulted in negative reactions, but when we repent ("I'm sorry") and ask for absolution ("Please forgive me"), the Source can erase the negative reactions. Our debts (our unpaid bills, or as yet unresolved issues with other people) are forgiven or cancelled if we, in turn, can forgive others. Even Jesus said: "Forgive us our trespasses, as we forgive those who trespass against us."

Everything Is Vibration

In the beginning was the word, the *logos,* the Big Bang, the sacred syllable *Aum* (*Om*). This world is sound, as everything is in vibration. There is no stasis in our universe; everything is vibrating, pulsating rhythmically, circling, and moving in cycles. What we call the status quo is only a snapshot in time, because at each moment hundreds of millions of biochemical reactions are taking place in every cell of our body. Sound is also mood and ambience: we often describe something as having a great atmosphere, good vibrations, or bad "vibes." We have an antenna for this and when we enter a room, we can sense where the "mood music" is coming from. Our universe is thus like a kind of giant symphony, and because everything is connected to everything else, everything also influences everything else, and *vice versa*. You and I are vibrating energy and frequencies, and everything manifests through the law of cause and effect, coming together through the law of resonance (*kuolo*).

Just as the crests of waves with the same vibration amplify one another, opposing and incompatible vibrations in perpetrator/victim relationships also come together and cancel each other out. Just how frequencies come together and amplify one another can be seen in teamwork, in a committed partnership, and in sport, of course; two people in a team are more than just two individuals, as they mutually inspire, challenge, and encourage one another. How out-of-synch vibrations cancel each other out, on the other hand, can be seen when work colleagues fail to see eye to eye. No matter what skills and ideas they bring to the table, both performance and enjoyment diminish as they get in each other's way and paralyze progress.

Every conflict, judgment, and condemnation, every moan and complaint leads to a reduction in energy levels ("I'm exhausted") and ultimately to dissonance and discord ("I just can't bear to listen any longer"). This disharmony, dissension, and disagreement is the opposite of love and leads to burnout, debts and bankruptcy, accidents and illness, divorce and separation ("I've just got to get out of here"). Medical science assumes mental, emotional, and physical stress to be the principal cause of many diseases. Harmony, sincere empathy, non-violence (Sanskrit: *ahimsa*) in all things, inner peace, forgiveness, and reconciliation lead to healing, health, and happiness, however. Since everything influences everything else, I personally contribute to harmony when I discover my share in disharmony and enter into the process of healing. I am a part of this world and, by healing myself, I take part in healing the world. These simple, clear connections between cause and effect, these resonances, show every individual just what possibilities and responsibilities are theirs.

Exercise: Inner Harmony

Take some time out for yourself and think about the situations that make you feel exhausted and unable to bear to listen to (or hear about) something any longer, or make you feel compelled to get out. What are you really struggling with?

1. For the first part of this exercise, make a note of everything concerning this situation, finally getting the issue out of your head and down onto paper. Ask yourself at what times you react with a fight-or-flight response instead of responding calmly. Write it all down and realize that there are experiences here that desire to be healed and set free. Life does not want bad things for us, instead it wishes to give us important gifts. The universe also knows, however, that we can only use these gifts when it gives

them to us in the form of experiences. We remember the things that hurt us and become aware of what is important through the contrast with those things that annoy and overwhelm us, or that we hate.

2. For the second part, make a note of what brings you pleasure. What is important to you, what feelings, sensations, and experiences do you wish to have? Set yourself free from the perpetrators and make a note of what you would like to feel.

3. Now thank both life and the perpetrator, as their role was to bring you to the point at which you became aware of your needs and desires.

4. Finally, connect in your heart with the perpetrator and the power of love within you. Now read the four sentences of the simplified Ho'oponopono and their explanation on page 60.

All Spirit Is God's Spirit

"In as much as ye have done it unto one of the least of these my brethren, ye have done it unto me."

Matthew 25:40

We are far more than our physical body and far more than our thoughts. We have a body, but we *are not* this body. We are also not our thoughts; we *have* thoughts, and they are often not even our own but instead, for example, a reaction to the headlines in a newspaper or mental programming handed down from our ancestors or absorbed from our culture. Even thinking is not as simple as all that; recent research at Stanford University has shown that while around three decades ago we used an average of around six to ten percent of our brain capacity in active thinking, today it is only three percent. This means that instead of primarily thinking, we react. What can we expect from ourselves and the world if we ignore the still, small voice of our hearts that always knows what is right, and instead wallow in negative news, in weeping and wailing, and fail to learn to forgive? If our greatest tool, our brain, is not used correctly, it will go to seed. I would maintain that we have the ability to reason in order to heal, to bless, and to prosper, not to destroy. And yet most people spend their time thinking about what they do not want rather than what they do want. This leaves them in conflict with themselves and with life. Life and the universe evolve as a creative process; neither ever asks itself what it does not want, but instead merely creates. In a Hoʻoponopono we seek out what we have in common, cleansing the negative and creating positivity.

We—you and me, animals and plants—are spiritual beings that use our bodies as a kind of vehicle. The driver of this physical vehicle, our true identity, is Spirit. Spirit does not age. It always was and always will be. This divine spark is a part of the eternal, loving, causeless Source known in Sanskrit as *atma,* and in our culture as *pneuma* or the soul. In Huna this concept is known as *kane,* which means "spirit of God's spirit." This understanding, that we are spiritual beings using our bodies as a means of transport, is common to many cultures. Just as all road users are the same, whether astride a bicycle, sitting on a tractor, or reclining in a sports car, all spiritual beings are the same as well, whether they happen to be making use of a human or an animal body. We might all look different, but all living creatures, from dolphins to butterflies and from blackbirds to ants, have equal worth. No one is stupid enough to believe deep down that they are a better person because they drive a smarter car, nor is any living creature better or worse than another because it possesses a different body. This is why you can't pet some animals while sending others to the slaughterhouse. You and I are not material beings that also have spiritual experiences, but quite the opposite; by nature, we are non-physical, spiritual creatures (*atma, pneuma,* soul, spirit) that are experiencing the world physically. It is our job as humans to use our reasoning capacity to protect the weak, the animals and plants that have no voice. It used to be that the strong protected the weak, treating Nature and all living creatures with respect and gratitude, before the terrible era of conflict began in which people condemn and fight one another over trivialities.

Huna and other spiritual traditions consider animals and plants as brothers and sisters, and Nature is revered as the Great Mother from whom we all come and by whom we are nourished. There is nothing insignificant or inferior in this world, all existence has a meaning. It is an expression of life in and of itself, and everything that exists comes together to form reality. The two syllables *re* and *al* derive from ancient Egyptian; *re* refers to "God" and *al* can be interpreted as "inherent, existent." In the language of priests, the word *real* described the all-pervading existence of the Divine, the notion that everything that exists originates from a single Source. This spiritual Source is within you, me, and everything that exists.

Meditation

I am sorry that I sometimes feel disillusioned and disappointed and so full of criticism, even though there is so much beauty in this world. I'm sorry for paying more attention to what is artificial than to, for example, the eternal sunrise. I'm sorry for listening to negative news more often than the glorious sound of a bee humming. I forgive myself for being trapped in a world full of artificial needs and for being discontented as a result. I am changing that now, by turning toward life and love. I love myself, and I love life. Thank you for healing all those involved in the here and now.

Exercise: Recognize Your Role

Think of a problem to do with environmental protection where you feel powerless and believe that there are people who are responsible for destroying Nature.

Visualize the full extent of the issue, terrible as it may well be. Connect with the people, animals, and plants, with Mother Earth, and the Source of all being (*pule*). Ask yourself what part you play or responsibility you have. What things do you do or use that contribute to this problem and justify the actions of the people involved? In what ways are you similar to them?

Look around your home, think about the contents of your wardrobe, your kitchen, or living room. What is there in your home that is contributing to destroying the environment? What are the raw materials and products that are responsible for allergies, illness, environmental destruction, the mass displacement of people and animals, death, and the extinction of life—all just for cheap profit and hedonism?

All of this represents your part of the greater drama, and is the second part of a Hoʻoponopono, the analysis and discussion phase (*mahiki*). Both your inner child (*unihipili*) and your higher self (*aumakua*) already know that you are indirectly involved, for example in experiments on animals (torture). As you are not in harmony with your conscious values, you experience inner conflict for which you may be trying to compensate. Forgive yourself unconditionally now, and pardon yourself and everyone else for your behavior (*mihi*). For each point that you have identified and made a note of, conduct a forgiveness ritual with the four sentences (*kala*) and rekindle the flame of *aloha*. This is a powerful Hoʻoponopono, as something is also healed on a higher level whenever we send new information onto the plane of general consciousness. Finally, if you are looking for ways in which to do something constructive for the natural world while avoiding the use of products that are harmful to the environment, the matter is *oki* and *pani*.

Hoʻoponopono in Practice

Relationships and Partnerships

We can agree that we humans have inherited a paradise. Just as we were given our bodies by our parents, and, on a higher level, by Mother Nature, we live on this Earth having had to do nothing: none of us made the water, the air, or the ground, and yet we somehow find it difficult to work together on our natural responsibility for preserving this paradise, the Earth.

As long as you live alone, you might think you are entirely affable and accommodating, but in a relationship, whether personal or professional (anywhere that things can get a bit "cramped"), people will soon notice your "quirks." Squeeze a tube of toothpaste and toothpaste will come out, and it's the same with people: whatever is inside will emerge as soon as they are challenged in a relationship. This is why relationships are valuable, as you recognize yourself in other people. Every problem, whether it's conflict, back pain, a loss of earnings, or environmental catastrophe, is a relationship problem to a certain extent. Everything is connected to, and has some kind of relationship with, everything else. If you have a sore back, ask yourself what relationships are involved that may directly or indirectly be responsible for this—your relationship with your body, your workplace, with the furniture you sit on, with your fears, with all kinds of things. Whether it's within a small or large *ohana,* within a marriage, a group of colleagues or humanity as a whole, forgoing our rivalries and cooperating seems to be a life lesson we have to learn.

Perhaps your partnership is an unhappy one or you have just ended a relationship and still have scars that need to be healed. As long we think about a relationship with anger, hatred, sorrow, or disappointment, our *aka* threads will stick fast and, because of the resonance principle, we will only ever attract a similar relationship or generally block ourselves from forming a new, harmonious, and loving relationship because we have not yet set ourselves free. If you don't heal the hurt from old relationships, partnerships, or in the workplace, history is very likely to repeat itself and the same thing is likely to happen to you again. Rage, hatred, and bitterness are strong feelings that ironically attract precisely the things and people at which they are directed. To find your dream partner or to have a dream relationship, you must first be a dream partner yourself, otherwise your partner or companion will say goodbye because you do not match their resonance.

Exercise: Set Yourself Free

Please forgive yourself, for example, for having stayed in a relationship that was bad for you. The good thing about this is that you now know better—so you're a winner! Set yourself free from your old partner on an energetic level, forgive them, and free yourself. Forgive yourself unconditionally and say farewell to all your feelings of guilt.

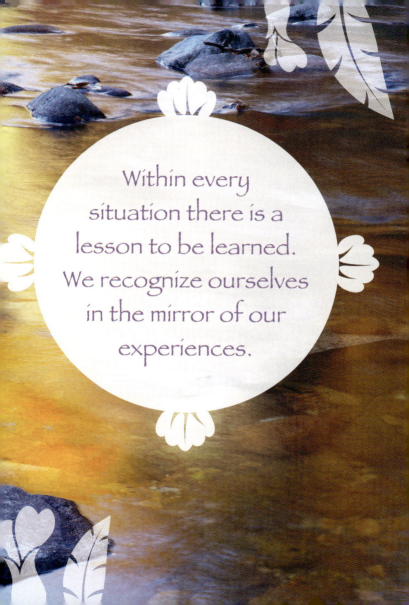

Within every situation there is a lesson to be learned. We recognize ourselves in the mirror of our experiences.

Profession, Vocation, and Remuneration

Choosing a meaningful professional role and the right place in which to work are crucial for our mental well-being. Just as a tree will grow as tall as it can, we want to do our best in life. We all have unique abilities and talents, assets that are our own contribution to the common good, the great *ohana*. This means that each of us carries a precious treasure within us: our individual vocation. Vocation means that we have a calling, a purpose, and when we follow this calling, everything will be right. We will then experience great inner contentment because we are holding nothing back. We are connected with everything and living in harmony with life, while our life is following a plan that is greater than us.

Meditation

I now accept myself unconditionally, with all my doubts and fears, and my uncertainty too. I love myself, with all my strengths and weaknesses. I forgive myself and ask for forgiveness from all those I have criticized because I was projecting my own inadequacy onto them. I'm sorry for hurting others through my own inadequacy. I honor and respect you. Thank you for healing all those involved.

Exercise: Acknowledge Your Dream

Imagine the following situation: You are lying on your deathbed and your talents enter the room. One after another, they approach your bed and ask why you failed to do more to develop them. "Why didn't you make more of me?" Perhaps you have a knack for languages, a flair for cooking exquisite dishes, or a gift for healing, but you allowed your skills to stagnate in a mediocre compromise. Finally, your dream, the one wish you always had, enters and asks: "Why did you forget me? I spoke to you every day. Why didn't you live me out?" You and your dream gently hold hands; what do you want to say to your dream in reply?

If you do not yet know your vocation, perhaps if you are unemployed or have a job that is wearing you down mentally and physically, forgive yourself. You may not be in exactly the right place, but resistance to a situation often only makes it even worse. Love and accept yourself and the situation, since we can only resolve and change what we have first accepted. I would strongly recommend that you set yourself goals and consistently focus on finding a solution. Make a decision and use Hoʻoponopono and meridian tapping (EFT) to remove anything that is preventing you from accepting your life's mission, such as feelings of guilt, doubts, and fears. Just when you turn toward life, it will come to your aid in what seems like a miraculous way.

Money is another topic that causes problems. It is an energy that seems to amplify a person's character. In our society, money is an expression of the value of our work but also of the value that we attribute to ourselves. A friend of mine charges an exceptionally high rate for his work as a gardener, "because I love myself," as he once told me with a grin, and he always gets first-rate commissions (from people, of course, who also love themselves and appreciate his work).

Start to appreciate yourself more and praise yourself. If you fail to value yourself, no one else will do so. You only get back in life what you think of yourself. Also think about how much you appreciate and show this appreciation to others; I can promise you that your whole life will move in a new and positive direction the moment you stop judging other people. The principle in this respect is "Judge not, that ye be not judged." (Matthew 7:1) Like a great ocean liner, your life will change course and you will travel to marvelous places.

Meditation

I'm sorry for judging myself and other people.

Please forgive me for having sown discord in the world. I forgive myself for this, and I now choose to let go of all self-accusation and to respect all living beings. Thank you for the healing of all those involved in the here and now.

Our self-image, family circumstances, patterns of behavior, and beliefs can all have an influence on our finances. If your bank balance seems to have hit a financial glass ceiling beyond which you cannot seem to pass, ask yourself what parallels exist within yourself. The first step is, of course, to ask whether you have deserved any reward at all, and if so what it might be. The second marker is the family. Do you allow yourself to earn more than your parents, or does it give you a bad feeling? The third indicator relates to the dynamics of your account—if your bank balance goes up and down, it raises the question as to whether you are volatile, unstable, and unreliable? Examine yourself, search your heart for the reason, and then forgive yourself and consider the following: studies in the United States have shown that, after three years, more than eighty percent of all American lotto millionaires found themselves back where they started financially before their big win. Our life circumstances are undoubtedly the result of our conditioning, which is why only what is within us can ever be manifested in the outside world. This is where Ho'oponopono and meridian tapping (EFT) can help, specifically allowing you to eliminate all the things that cause you to fail, and to change your conditioning for the positive.

Health

Jesus of Nazareth is considered the greatest healer in Christian biblical world history. He healed the blind, the lame, the insane, and many others. But in the Bible stories, he always emphasizes that he was not the one who healed the people, but rather it was their own faith. We become healthy and are healed the moment we recognize our perfection and perform this paradigm shift. This may happen spontaneously or require a little practice. As long as we remain convinced that we do not deserve anything good (because in our own eyes, we have made mistakes), nothing good will be able to come to us either. The wall around our heart cannot be breached without self-forgiveness and self-love, so keep working with the four sentences in your thoughts and free your heart of old wounds. Please forgive yourself unconditionally.

In Hawaiian culture, all physical healing would be preceded by a Ho'oponopono in a Hawaiian temple. Our minds shape matter and before the body can be healed (Hawaiian: *kino*, "the dark shadow"), the mind must also be healed. As Hippocrates (460–370 BCE), another great physician in world history, commented,

"There are no incurable diseases, only incurable people." Healing means becoming complete, but how can we be complete when we reject something within us, perhaps our body, our habits, or our past? When we are ill, something is missing, but it is not our health that is lacking but our belief in and trust in our perfection.

Exercise: Trust in Your Own Worth

Now express this with the following powerful affirmation: "I am ready to learn and to improve myself, but I am already perfectly worthy, even now, before I have learned this lesson." Keep repeating this sentence, especially when you are feeling guilty or someone is trying to control you by denigrating you. Always remember that you are a part of the perfect Source and that the Divine within you sees only perfection. On the other hand, your energy will flow to whatever you see. In Huna we call this energy principle *makia*. Make a decision to let go of all negative emotions and use your inner peace to make a consistent and active contribution toward activating your powers of self-healing.

After discovering the connection between mind and body, Louise L. Hay (author and founder of Hay House) published the classic *Heal Your Body* in 1976. Her findings were put to the greatest test when she contracted cancer. In a later interview about her film, *You Can Heal Your Life: The Movie,* Louise explains how she healed her cancer with consistent physical and mental detoxification. The challenge and test for her was to let go of all the traumatic experiences of her childhood and unconditionally to forgive all those who were involved. In her therapeutic work, she had come to realize that most illnesses and problems disappeared as soon as her clients began to accept, forgive, and love themselves. If you fail to forgive yourself for the mistakes of the past and think you are guilty, you will become ill. After all, one of the things that our culture programs into us most forcefully is that we must be punished and suffer for mistakes. It is quite simple; if you keep blaming yourself for something, you are programming your subconscious mind, the lower self (*ku*), for destruction. You will then eat too much or too little, sleep too much or too little, perhaps work until you drop, or start trying to please everybody. People store up mental and emotional stress for themselves with their self-accusations and criticism, and since this stress is long-term, they become ill.

The Global Political Challenge

*"I am part of this world.
When I change,
the world changes with me."*

Native Americans say that if one person in a family has a problem, it is everyone's problem, and the same applies on a national and global level. Thanks to the internet, and to ever speedier means of transport that allow us easy access to almost anywhere in the world, the world is shrinking. We can see great challenges ahead: conflict caused by religious differences, energy and banking crises, never-ending rivers of blood from slaughterhouses, poverty and global hunger, environmental catastrophes, and more besides. And *last, but not least,* for the last fifty years, we have been producing something in amounts that are now threatening to engulf us—trash. We are wasting our lives in trying to find the meaning of life in the trivial. We are throwing our lives in the trash; just like the many small, meaningless objects in which we find short-term pleasure but which are based on exploiting the Earth's riches, we are throwing our lives away too.

What can any one individual do? What can you or I do? How can we get out of this tangle of emotions, and stop feeling powerless and thinking like a victim ("There's nothing I can do anyway")? I am convinced we can do a great deal, and when we are in harmony with our values, we will have no feelings of guilt about not doing what, at the bottom of our hearts, we feel to be right.

Exercise: Improve the World

If something is bothering you, if you want to improve a situation, or bring something on this Earth into harmony, ask yourself the following four questions.

1. What is the problem?
2. What is my part in the problem?
3. What can I do to make things better?
4. How can I set an example and in so doing inspire others?

Explore the part you play in the matter, and think about how and where you are involved on the various relationship levels, taking into consideration your behavior toward people, animals, plants, and the natural world as a whole.

Now conduct a Ho'oponopono to cleanse all the negativity, the thoughts causing the problems, and the behaviors that are preventing you from being "the change that you wish to see in the world," a quote often credited to Indian leader Mahatma Gandhi. Say and feel what you are sorry about and what you wish to apologize to Mother Earth for. Ask for forgiveness and listen to the answer in your heart. In your mind, bow your head and say "I love you." Unconditionally forgive all those who through ignorance or complacency are harming the Earth, recognizing that you too often act unwittingly in many ways and thereby sow negativity. Give thanks for love, insight, and healing, and for help in being able to change something and so play a part in healing the world.

When you have moved yourself—and thus the world—a small step away from destruction and back toward love, seek out ways for peace, at work or at home, in your diet, and in your habits as a consumer in particular. What companies do you support, directly or indirectly, that are involved in the ruthless destruction and cruel exploitation of people and animals? Ask yourself if there were something you could do to be part of the solution, what might it be?

Use your free will as a human being to increase the good in the world.

When you and I fully grasp just what can be achieved by faith in ourselves and in goodness, and what love and forgiveness can do, we have a powerful tool with which to steer world events for the better. Take the special property of holographic images; if you were to cut a hologram into smaller sections and examine one of them, however small, with a magnifying glass, you would still see the entire image. Put metaphysically, the part is the same as the whole, and vice versa. I maintain that we are living in a kind of cosmic hologram. Our actions have an effect everywhere. Take a single step toward harmony and peace and the whole world takes a step closer to harmony and peace. Each person needs only to start with themselves.

The mighty sun once asked, "Who will shine?" No one spoke and silence reigned. "I will be leaving soon, who will shine in my place?" said the sun once again, in a commanding tone. No one dared to say a word. Then the sun asked a third time: "Who will brighten the night when I am gone?"

"Me, I shall do it." Everyone looked up. Who had spoken?

The great sun asked, "Who are you?"

And the voice answered, "I am a candle."

"Where will you shine, and for how long?" asked the sun, its interest piqued.

The candle then plucked up courage and spoke: "I shall burn for exactly one night and light up a whole room." When the others heard this, a sea of candles began to shine, star by star.

The mighty sun nodded in contentment and spoke: "Good. Now I see myself in all of you and I realize I can leave, and shine once again tomorrow."

The Desire for Peace

One of the reasons behind our desire to solve problems in life is to be happy once more. Another is to find our peace (*malu*) and an even higher goal is reconciliation, when we put everything and everyone back in their rightful place and accord them their absolute value once more.

Every family conference begins and ends with a *pule:* I ask and give thanks for peace with people, peace with animals, peace with plants, peace with the Earth, peace with the cosmos, peace with God, and peace with myself.

This is known as the sevenfold peace, in which they all work together in the great *ohana,* in the ecosystem, and the cosmos (from the Greek word for harmony). There is nothing inferior in God's creation. Everything is important, and peace is an expression of this love, guaranteeing our free personal growth.

The teachings of the ancient Hawaiian shamans were harnessed to develop positive strengths in order for life circumstances to be formulated in harmony with everything-that-is. The shamans were known as *kahunas,* since a *kahu* is principally a guardian or keeper of royal values. Ask yourself what you want to preserve? What should be protected on Mother Earth? What do you stand for? The answers to these questions may offer some hint as to your calling in life.

It is time to delve a little deeper into how we can work together to keep the peace. Key to this is the Golden Rule that we should treat others as we would wish to be treated ourselves. However, this rule has far-reaching consequences, including for our behavior as consumers, for example.

When we encounter problems or obstacles, in a Hoʻoponopono, we always approach them from two angles: first, resolving the immediate problem, and then its causes. While these may be rooted far back in the past, their resolution can nip a host of future problems in the bud. What will really take us to the heart of the matter are our conscious or unconscious memories, "data" in the collective unconscious, programming from our ancestors, and personal harm sustained in the womb or in early childhood. The list of possible causes for our personal, national, and global problems is also a long one, but these can ultimately be boiled down to earlier wrongdoing.

Essentially, life on this beautiful planet could offer abundance, joy, and rich fellowship, but like viruses on a computer, disruptive programs exist within us that produce unwanted distortions and outcomes. These programs, trauma, and destructive paradigms transform potentially joyful life into a collective drama, resulting in misunderstandings and wrongdoing, such as exploitation, deceit, violence, abuse, and discord. Instead of each word and action being an expression of love, in conflict we experience calls for help and cries for love.

In a Ho'oponopono we look for all these unresolved elements within us. We cleanse our hearts, the center of our strength (*mana maka*), in order to send new and important information out into the *ohana* and the Earth's plane of general consciousness.

To achieve peace, the first, and very practical, step involves forgiving the following four parties: first, your parents; secondly, all your ex-partners; thirdly, everyone else; and fourthly, yourself. We forgive what we can and in forgiving others become our own rescuers. In forgiving ourselves, we redeem ourselves and forgiveness becomes an act of self-love and liberation.

Forgiveness does not strive to turn a wrong into a right, nor does it mean allowing someone to harm you.

Making peace means finding reconciliation in your heart. On the higher level of the inner sciences, this reconciliation symbolizes the homecoming of lost daughters and sons. Although we ourselves have many faults, we still want to reproach our sisters and brothers for theirs, but this demeans us and distances us from our souls. Through our homecoming to a spiritual paradise, and in regaining our awareness of our spiritual connection and unity, we shall regain our dignity.

A warrior once sought out a wise old woman because he was being tormented by the spirits of his slain enemies. "Tell me, dear lady, is there hope for me? Is there a heaven and a hell? Where shall I go?" The

shaman replied: "Why should I share this wisdom with a coward like you?" The young warrior fell into a rage at being spoken to in such a manner and, quick as lightning, drew his sword to cut off the wise old woman's head. However, she stayed his hand with a simple gesture, saying calmly: "My son, what you are feeling right now is hell." He then lowered his sword and began to weep bitter tears. "And that, my son," said the wise old woman, gently, "that is heaven."

In this new era, we may understand that war or conflict, whether within ourselves, in our partnership or marriage, at work, or between nations, may lose its significance, as it proves that we are still not advanced, emotionally mature individuals. It's easy to destroy something, to trade blows, or to shoot someone. Any fool can do that, but to preserve something, to unite in love for the greater good of all requires real strength.

It is always glorious when we manage to overcome our inner demons. When we gaze in self-reflection at the mirror that the world holds up to us, the real enemy is less likely to be found outside than to be sought within ourselves.

To play your part in making peace, you will need positive strengths and to be at peace yourself. To be at peace, you need to have peace; to have peace, you need to become a source of peace yourself, and to become a source of peace, you must connect with the Source of all peace. Aloha.

For Healing

I am sorry that there was so much discord within me in the past. I ask forgiveness. Please forgive me if I or my ancestors have hurt you or your ancestors in any incarnation, either consciously or unconsciously. I love you and I thank you for this healing.

I now forgive each and every creature that has ever hurt me or my ancestors, either consciously or unconsciously, from the beginning of time to the present day, from the center of the universe to the most distant point. I love you all. I forgive you all and set you free. Thank you. Thank you. I give thanks for this miracle, as well as for the healing of all those involved in the here and now.

About the Author

Ulrich Emil Duprée has been teaching Ho'oponopono, the Hawaiian method of conflict resolution, to enthusiastic audiences since undergoing a mystical initiation by a kahuna, a Hawaiian shaman. His bestselling book *Ho'oponopono: The Hawaiian Forgiveness Ritual* has been translated into sixteen languages so far. By placing emphasis on the practical and on self-help, Ulrich teaches effective ways of applying this spiritual discipline.

His gift for combining relevant techniques from different spiritual and non-spiritual practices distinguishes him from other teachers in this field.

As he explains in the book, he teaches people how to heal different kinds of relationships.

One of Ulrich's special skills is showing people how they can forgive themselves and others in an effective way. As a result, the participants of his seminars make tremendous progress in all aspects of their lives.

If you're looking for advice or for more information, please see his English language website:

ulrich-dupree.com

Picture Credits

Page 5: Steener; pp. 6–7, 12, 48, 57: elena moiseeva; p. 7 frangipani flower: Nipaporn Panyacharoen; p. 10: Kryvenok Anastasiia; p. 13: ver0nicka; p. 20: Kichigin; p. 29: Madison McGinnis; p. 31: Erik Wollo; p. 44: Rock and Wasp; pp. 45, 47: Galyna Andrushko; p. 52: Romvy; pp. 62, 91: huyangshu; p. 66: goodeeday; p. 67: Lance Sagar; p. 76: Chechotkin; p. 87: GaudiLab; p. 96: Mizin Roman; p. 104: Elenamiv; p. 108: Yuriy Kulik. All shutterstock.com. Throughout: floral ornaments, decorative leaf: Telnov Oleksii/shutterstock.com

---

For further information and to request a book catalogue contact:
Inner Traditions, One Park Street, Rochester, Vermont 05767

Earthdancer Books is an Inner Traditions imprint.
Phone: +1-800-246-8648, customerservice@innertraditions.com
www.earthdancerbooks.com • www.innertraditions.com

EARTHDANCER

AN INNER TRADITIONS IMPRINT